Cycling – A Year Ro

D0309783

CYCLING

A YEAR ROUND PLAN

PAUL VAN DEN BOSCH

MEYER
& MEYER
SPORT

Original title: Het complete trainingshandboek voor de wielrenner
© 2001 by Zuidnederlandse Uitgeverij N.V., Aartselaar, Belgium

British Library Cataloguing in Publication Data
A catalogue record for this book is available from the British Library

Cycling – A Year Round Plan
Oxford: Meyer & Meyer Sport (UK) Ltd., 2006
ISBN 10: 1-84126-176-9
ISBN 13: 978-1-84126-176-8

© 2006 by Meyer & Meyer Sport (UK) Ltd.
Aachen, Adelaide, Auckland, Budapest, Graz, Johannesburg,
New York, Olten (CH), Oxford, Singapore, Toronto
Member of the World
Sports Publishers' Association (WSPA)
www.w-s-p-a.org
Printed and bound by: B.O.S.S Druck und Medien GmbH, Germany
ISBN 10: 1-84126-176-9
ISBN 13: 978-1-84126-176-8
E-Mail: verlag@m-m-sports.com
www.m-m-sports.com

INDEX

INTRODUCTION

It's been proven over and over. The ratings of live broadcasts, the thousands of viewers who populate the track of the classics and of the great cycle races regardless of weather considerations, the adoration for champions who have long since laid down their bikes, and the endless admiration of today's champions: no question cycling is one of the great passions of the people.

Young cyclists thus dream of following in the footsteps of their idols, in spite of the damned cobblestones of the north, in spite of the high peaks which quite evilly try to hoard the oxygen for which the cyclist yearns, and in spite of those damned moments of breaking away that cause the thighs to explode. They hope to capture some part of the glamour of the big champions—because that is what has become of professional sports and its huge piles of money: glamour and glitter.

These young cyclists once were assisted by coaches of various standards who were, by word of mouth only, acquainted with several methods and means to reach the ultimate goal. Back then, more than nowadays, it boiled down to the fact that the one who was able to kick the pedals the strongest and for the longest time would come the longest way. Talent and stamina, that was what it was about.

No one doubts the fact that these former champions could also be contemporary champions, albeit with less superiority. To a great extent, guidance from many sources has erased much of the difference between the talented and and the less talented.

Guidance of a cyclist has leapt from a medieval to a high tech period in just a couple of years. Whereas the cyclist used to be on his own, or a sports counselor used to give advice—often not so bad—from his gut feeling, physicians, dieticians, psychologists and physical trainers have their advice ready nowadays. Maximal oxygen uptake, anaerobic threshold, supercompensation, amount of ferritine, energy drinks etc. all slowly become part of the everyday vocabulary of each cyclist who takes their trade somewhat seriously. Cycling has become, in spite of its common characteristic, a rather complicated sport. A cyclist thus needs guidelines.

This book is my attempt to offer such guidelines, to amateurs and pros as well as trainers. The aim is to shed some light on the most important aspects of cycle training, especially from a practical point of view. The first chapters try to follow the preparation of a cyclist chronologically, starting from the end of the competition by mid-October till the beginning of the competition.

This period is the most important one regarding preparation.

Items covered are:

- How does a cyclist set up their training
- What about strength training
- How to determine the training intensity

These items are fully illustrated with examples of training schedules.

The reader will soon notice that using a heart rate monitor will be of capital importance. Next climbing training, sprint training and time trail training will be dealt with as well, not only from a theoretical point of view, but also practically speaking.

Questions about overtraining are answered. Special attention is given to the nutrition of the cyclist, before, during and after the ride. It is strange that this aspect, which is so important to reach the individual maximum performance level, is not well known enough or is wrongly assessed or considered as being not important by many cyclists and counselors.

I realize that one ideal training schedule does not exist. Training advice that differs from what the reader will be offered on the next pages is not better or worse by definition. Wether or not you reach the top is not only determined by the training done, but also by serveral other factors, like talent and mental strength.

One thing for sure: the training advice covered in this book has already proven its soundness, both for many of the best amateurs in Belgium and for lots of professionals.

This book is the result of thorough knowledge of cycling training through study, extensive experience, and with the cooperation and insights of Valerio Piva, former Italian cyclist with 12 years of professional experience on the biggest Italian teams. Also very useful has been the advice from the training staff of the MAPEI team.

Finally, I have spent many hours listening to the cyclists and continuously evaluating and adapting their training schedules based on their results to arrive at this final result. Use their experiences, pick the things you feel comfortable with, and your performances will get better.

Good luck!

Paul Van Den Bosch

CHAPTER 1

15 OCTOBER–30 NOVEMBER

The long and back-breaking competitive season usually finishes during the second half of October. An average professional racing cyclist easily enters 100 races or even more a year, among which are on average 5 to 10 smaller or larger stage races. The racing program of an amateur is more limited. He generally cycles 40 to 60 races per year. The best-organized amateur teams even take part in multiple stage races, in their own country and abroad.

Tests at the end of the competitive season indicate that accompanying fatigue can sometimes be situated in a cyclist's mental state, even more so than in physical health.

Physical recovery is often easier than mental recovery. Running over and over again in the mind is a film of not only successes, but also of errors and missed chances. Unfinished contract negotiations gone awry can also disturb the vital peace of mind.

Therefore it is advisable to first take leave after the last race, preferably spending time with family members or with friends with whom you can talk about other subjects than cycling.

Should all physical activity be stopped?

Certainly not. Stopping physical efforts too suddenly is not advisable. During the first week after the competition you should be "de-trained," then afterwards it is necessary to remain slightly physically active. Sports (for example swimming) undoubtedly will have a beneficial influence. These activities should, however, never be considered as training, but rather as active relaxing.

A lot of questions about this alternative exercising of sports often arise. Are sports such as running, squash, football, etc. during recovery or during the first part of the preparation stage advisable or inadvisable for a cyclist?

Cycling is a cyclic movement which is relatively quite harmless for the muscles. As a result, muscle ache, (also called muscle stiffness and not to be confused with muscle fatigue), rarely appears after cycling training, not even after an extremely intense effort such as a mount race concerning several cols. The cause of muscle ache is frequently found in very small muscle injuries (microtraumata) that appear after hard contact with the subsoil, especially if the athlete is not used to this. This therefore often occurs in sports in which the base is running. The risk of injuries must always be kept in mind when choosing some form of alternative exercise. From this point of view squash, and certainly soccer, is being dissuaded. Moreover a cyclist must, as soon as the actual preparation to the new competitive season starts, train **specifically**, i.e. on the bicycle. That is why alternative exercise only belongs to the relative recovery period and never to a specific form of training. It should be used as a means to actively recover from the past efforts.

How long does this recovery period last?

The answer to this question is stipulated by a number of factors such as:

- How tough was the race season, both psychologically and mentally?

- When is the first main point of the coming racing season situated?

- Does the cyclist "yearn for the bicycle"?

The recovery period generally starts around 15 October. On average it can be stated that this resting period must last three to four weeks.

During the first days of the first week you still cycle a bit to actively recover from the last race. Afterwards there are more or less three weeks in which the bike should be put away. This is the ideal period to really take some time off. Cyclists can already start alternative sports during this period, in each case at a very moderate level.

During the third week of November training is gradually resumed. Cyclists start purely on their instincts–short and light endurance training sessions in which suppleness is emphasized. A series of four training rides of approximately two hours is more than enough for this first week. A lot of cyclists opt for the mountain bike at this stage of preparation. In itself this should not be condemned, but the risk of too high training intensity becomes more likely because the cyclist mostly rides in a hilly area. A heart rate monitor, which gives a very thorough idea of the real training intensity, can be an excellent device in this case. This subject I will elaborate on further.

In addition to these easy endurance training sessions, cyclists must as soon as possible tackle strength training.

Strength training

Modern cycling has evolved, especially during the last decade, into an endurance discipline in which strength will always play a larger role. That is why a considerable amount of strength training belongs in the training program of every cyclist seriously involved with his profession.

The training element "strength" can be subdivided into several components, such as maximum strength, explosive strength and strength endurance on the one hand, and dynamic strength and static strength on the other hand.

Maximum strength means the maximum resistance which can be overcome in one recurrence by developing maximum muscle tension in the muscle fibers.

Explosive strength is reached by the maximum muscle tension which can be developed in the muscle fibers in the shortest possible time. In other words, an external resistance must be overcome with the largest possible contraction speed.

Strength endurance is defined as the capacity of repeating a relatively light strength effort during a certain time. This training element can still be differently defined as the capacity against fatigue in long-term strength efforts of relatively low intensity in a dynamic pattern.

Dynamic strength training implies that while developing muscle tension the muscle length changes, either shortens (which is called concentric contraction), or extends (which is called excentric contraction).

Static strength training means that while developing muscle tension the muscle length does not change. The strength is, in other words, displayed in relation to a fixed resistance.

It should be clear that a cyclist especially benefits from developing strength endurance in a dynamic pattern. Static strength training must absolutely be avoided, because the–initially fast–increase of strength rapidly stabilizes, but the profit in muscle volume is not paired with an increase of the muscle capillarisation (capillary vessels around the muscles). Static muscle training is too unspecific and has a negative impact on local muscle endurance.

How does this strength training actually work?

Strength training in the gym

Strength training in the gym has several advantages. The winter period is, of course, not the most pleasant one to constantly train outdoors. To cyclists, indoor strength training means a necessary supplement to the cycling training in which a general conditioning training diagram can be completed under pleasant circumstances. Leg muscles specifically are not the only ones trained, but the other large muscle groups of the body as well. If you do this together with other cyclists, this contact can be motivating.

It is very important that every cyclist gets a strength training program using a workload which has been established by means of certain individual data. This means that every strength exercise must be worked with a percentage of the maximum workload which can be overcome by the cyclist in that specific exercise going through the complete movement range. This is called **1 RM**, or one repetition maximum.

In the first stage a **general strength training program** must be completed. Therefore 1RM must be stipulated for several exercises using every large muscle group of the body: the scapula muscles, the shoulder muscles (delta muscles), the biceps muscle, the triceps, the chest muscles, the hamstrings, the quadriceps and the calf muscles. To train the abdomen muscles it is not necessary to determine 1RM in advance.

Determination of 1RM

Determining 1RM is a very straining process, because one should strive for the maximum workload. Therefore some strict rules must be met:

- A good general warm-up (running, cycling, stepping or rowing);

- A good specific warm-up of the muscle group mobilized;

- A correct implementation of the exercises.

After a good general and specific warming-up, 1RM is determined in a maximum of three steps.

One starts at a workload which still can be overcome fairly easily. Instinctively the load is still raised two times to the real maximum workload which can be overcome. The correct implementation is of vital importance because during bad implementation, compensation movements are made. This means that muscle groups other than the ones intended will be activated during the implementation of the movement. The efficiency of the strength exercise gets lost because of this, and the compensation movements often lead to overload injuries. Therefore it is important to firstly learn the strength exercises guided by an expert using a light workload. From this point of view it should be clear that working with fitness tools is preferred to strength training with weights.

Training strength endurance

If 1RM is determined for the various exercises one should first of all pay attention to the improvement of **strength endurance**. The development of this strength endurance is an absolutely necessary foundation for later training of maximum strength.

Strength endurance is developed by means of a large number of repetitions to 40 to 50% of 1RM. In a traditional training pattern lasting more or less eight weeks, a set-up of 30 to 100 repetitions is suggested.

To obtain optimum training impact, two to three training sessions a week are required. You must take into account, however, that there must be at least one recovery day between two sessions, since the muscle development during and after the training session reduces, but reaches a prime 24 hours later.

Training maximum strength

After five weeks of strength endurance training you can start training at **maximum strength** the most important muscles used specifically for cycling, viz. the knee stretchers (quadriceps).

Maximum strength training is not appropriate for the other large muscle groups because this only leads to non-functional strength profit and weight increase. Training of the maximum strength for a cyclist requires a workload of 70 to 75% of 1RM. The number of repetitions and series is lower than for the strength endurance training and the recovery period lasts longer.

A general strength training diagram can look like this:

week	muscle group	Repetitions	% 1 RM	Recovery between series
1	all	3x10	40-50%	30"
2	all	3x12	40-50%	30"
3	all	4x10	40-50%	30"
4	all	4x12	40-50%	30"
5	• all • quadriceps	• 5x12 • 3x6	• 40-50% • 70%	• 30" • 2'-3'
6	• all • quadriceps	• 5x15 • 4x6	• 40-50% • 70%	• 30" • 2'-3'
7	• all • quadriceps	• 5x17 • 4x7	• 40-50% • 70%	• 30" • 2'-3'
8	• all • quadriceps	• 5x20 • 4x8	• 40-50% • 75%	• 30" • 2'-3'

Because strength training in the gym is non-specific, you should try to ride the ergometer bicycle 5 to 10 minutes after every leg exercise. After strength training, cycle about half an hour on the rollers or at least one hour on the road. The objective is to transfer the strength profit obtained to the specific muscle function of the cycling movement.

leg press (m. quadriceps)

calfs

lat pulley (back)

leg curl (hamstrings)

sitting rowing (back)

half squat (m. quadriceps)

triceps press down (m. triceps)

bench press (m. pectoralis)

crunches (abdominals)

biceps curl (m. biceps)

m. gluteus

Stretching

Stretching should be done before and after doing weight training to avoid stiff and sore muscles. When you do it before weight training, you should warm up carefully to warm up the muscles and to lubricate the joints. Stretch one muscle group at the time, and stretch to mild tension. Don't bounce, because bouncing engages the "stretch reflex".

Some essential stretches for the lower body:

Stretching of the ilio-tibial tract

Stretching of the m. gluteï and the hamstrings

Stretching of the hamstrings

Stretching of the hamstrings and the adductors of the thigh

Stretching of the hamstrings and the adductors of the thigh

Stretching of the m. gluteï and the lower back

Stretching of the muscles of the calf

Stretching of the quadriceps

Specific strength training

Specific strength training means the **strength training on the bicycle**, cycling on an ergometer bicycle or on rollers having adjustable resistance. This resistance is established so that the cyclist, always sitting on the saddle, must push hard to make 40 to 60 rotations per minute. Strictly speaking the threshold (see further on) must not be exceeded during this training. Searching for the correct resistance in which the heart rate increases not too dramatically is not easy in an early stage. It demands some experience and searching before the specific strength training is carried out as it should be.

Concerning the number of rotations/minute during the strength training, opinions differ greatly. One point of view keeps it on 60 rot./min. More rotations is hardly to be called strength training, less rotations would be too non-specific, i.e. too far remote from reality. Another point of view opts for 40 rot./min, because this would allow better recovering after the training.

This training can considerably strain the knee tendons, which is why the cyclist should build up the training workload very gradually.

Building up training:

Week	Duration (minutes)	Repetitions	Recovery (minutes)
1	2	3	2
2	2	4	2
3	2	5	2
4	3	4	3
5	3	5	3
6	3	6	3
7	3	7	3
8	3	8	3

Strength training on rollers always starts with a warm-up of at least 15 minutes, in which you cycle at 100–120 and even more rotations per minute.

During the recovery periods as well you cycle relaxed at a high pedaling frequency and at a low heart rate. In this case as well it is recommended to smoothly cycle 1 to 2 hours on the road with low gear ratio or 30 to 60 minutes on the rollers after the specific strength training. These suppleness training sessions on the rollers are also necessary to obtain good coordination, helping the cyclist learn to develop a high pedaling frequency. These speed training sessions are important as a base for possible sprint training sessions.

Note:

The transfer to a new team will often be paired with change of bicycle, pedals and bicycle shoes. Thus one should strive for a bicycle position which is as much as possible identical to the old bicycle position. This generally is still realizable. The transfer to new shoes and pedals is far more difficult. This change must be gradual, i.e. one cannot train immediately at full strength with the new material. Possibly you should vary with the familiar material in the beginning. You should be especially careful with the specific strength training. To avoid injuries a cyclist must be adapted 100% to the new material before he starts this kind of training.

Change of bicycle position must always be very gradual. If a cyclist decides to raise his saddle just 1 cm, this must be done progressively, each time in stages of no more than 3 mm maximum.

Training with a fixed gear

During the preparation period, training regularly with fixed gear is ideal. In a first stage you cycle to low gear ratio, for example 42x17. As the preparation period progresses, gear ratio can become gradually higher, until eventually you cycle to a gear ratio of 52x16. The cyclist should not be afraid to also train on a hilly track at fixed gear. The scope of the training is built up from 1/2 hour to even 3 to 4 hours (in a later stage of the preparation period), and two to three times per week.

Which are the advantages of such training sessions?
First of all the output of these training sessions is much higher. You pedal constantly, and as a result the training heart rate can be easily kept at an even level.

Furthermore such training sessions, especially when training at sufficiently low gear ratio, are very favorable for the suppleness. Eventually the combination of strength and suppleness is one of the most important objectives during the preparation period. Anyone who saw Armstrong climb the mountains during the Tour de France immediately understands the importance of this combination.

Training at fixed gear is not harmless and demands great concentration. Riding bends is paired with a certain risk and stopping suddenly is not always obvious. That is why it is advised to do this training on quiet roads.

Examples

Week 1

Day	Training	Type	Description
Monday	1	Strength training	General strength training 50% 1RM 3x10 repetitions, rec. 30 sec
	2	Suppleness	60 min easy riding on the road, 42 x 17-18 or 30 min easy riding on rollers
Tuesday	1	Aerobic endurance training Suppleness	90 min fixed gear 42 x 16-18
Wednesday	1	strength training	General strength training 50% 1RM 3x10 repetitions, rec. 30 sec
	2	Suppleness	60 min easy riding on the road, 42 x 17-18 or 30 min easy riding on rollers
Thursday	1	Aerobic endurance training Suppleness	90 min fixed gear 42 x 16-18
Friday	1	Strength training	Specific strength training 30 min rollers with 3 x 2 min resistance, 40-60 rot./min. Heart rate never above threshold rec. 2 min easy riding.
	2	Suppleness	60 min easy riding on the road, 42 x 17-18 or 30 min easy riding on rollers
Saturday	1	Aerobic endurance training Suppleness	90 min fixed gear 42 x 16-18
Sunday			Recovery

Week 2

Day	Training	Type	Description
Monday	1	Strength training	General strength training 50% 1RM 3x12 repetitions, rec. 30 sec
	2	Suppleness	75 min easy riding on the road, 42 x 17-18 or 45 min easy riding on rollers
Tuesday	1	Aerobic endurance training Suppleness	90 min fixed gear 42 x 16-18
Wednesday	1	Strength training	General strength training 50% 1RM 3x12 repetitions, rec. 30 sec
	2	Suppleness	75 min easy riding on the road, 42 x 17-18 or 45 min easy riding on rollers
Thursday	1	Aerobic endurance training Suppleness	90 min fixed gear 42 x 16-18
Friday	1	Strength training	Specific strength training 30 min rollers with 3 x 2 min resistance, 40-60 rot./min. rec. 2 min easy riding. Never above threshold.
	2	Suppleness	75 min easy riding on the road, 42 x 17-18 or 45 min easy riding on rollers
Saturday	1	Aerobic endurance training Suppleness	120 min fixed gear 42 x 16-18
Sunday			Recovery

CHAPTER 2

1 DECEMBER–31 DECEMBER

The main objectives of this period are:

- Gradually building up the strength training, both in the gym and on the bicycle
- Gradually building up the training volume on the road
- Keeping emphasis on suppleness and strength
- Introducing more intensive training stimuli from time to time
- Determining the correct training intensity for the different types of training

The different types of training

Recovery training

Recovery training is carried out in order to recover from preceding training sessions. The intensity is very low, and the training volume limited. These training sessions have a favorable impact on removing the waste products in the muscles and they are generally preferred to passive recovery. The importance of the recovery training is underestimated by a lot of cyclists. You should train hard in order to obtain results, but the eventual training impact can be only realized during the (active) recovery period.

A real recovery training session never lasts longer than 30 to 90 minutes. A lot of cyclists are inclined to still cycle 2 to 3 hours at a low intensity on recovery days. This is too long to obtain complete recuperation. In bad weather it is advisable to carry out the recovery training on rollers. Training in cold, rain and wind requires extra energy from the body and blocks good recuperation.

The aerobic endurance training

The perfect means to reach your aerobic endurance capacity is **aerobic endurance training**. This type of endurance is the most important physical characteristic that a cyclist should develop because it forms the base for all other more intensive training types. In aerobic endurance capacity training, oxygen provides the kind of energy which is necessary to keep up the effort. This oxygen burns the two large energy reserves in the body, viz. fatty acids and carbohydrates. During the oxidation of these energy sources, much energy is being released, but it lasts a while before the energy supply gets going. The aerobic endurance capacity mainly serves efforts of relatively low intensity and considerably long duration. "Relatively" indicates that the cyclist's degree of training must be taken into account. What is a low intensity to a cyclist of high level, could mean a high intensity for an amateur cyclist.

The difference between energy which is provided by the oxidation of carbohydrates and the energy which is provided by the oxidation of fatty acids is important.

The fat store in the body is much larger than the carbohydrate store, but you need more oxygen to obtain the same amount of energy from the oxidation of fatty acids than from the oxidation of carbohydrates. Hence that during a very intense effort the carbohydrate store will be first addressed.

For example: the energy for a time trial is almost entirely provided by the oxidation of carbohydrates. During a race however we generally face paces in which energy is partly provided by oxidation of fatty acids, and partly by oxidation of carbohydrates. As the intensity rises, the share of carbohydrate oxidation becomes larger.

When this supply is exhausted (after approximately 90 minutes of intense effort) the body switches to oxidation of fatty acids. This moment of switching is known among cyclists as "the man with the hammer" or "the wall". Cyclists therefore should be so well trained that they can overcome the first and largest part of the race on their fat metabolism, so that they can enter the final, when pace becomes dramatically higher, using their still-untouched carbohydrate store. Of course in breakaways and accelerations during the first part of the race the carbohydrate store is inevitably already addressed. Therefore it is necessary to replenish this store by means of energy drinks at the beginning of the race. By training, the switching of fatty acids to carbohydrates can be influenced. This subject will be further elaborated.

VO$_2$max

The aerobic endurance capacity of the cyclist is often indicated by the **maximal oxygen uptake (VO$_2$max)**. This parameter indicates how much oxygen can be incorporated in the fibers (mainly the active muscles) of the cyclist at maximum effort. **VO$_2$max** considered absolutely is expressed in liters per minute. Because a very muscular cyclist can take in more oxygen than a light cyclist with less muscle mass, **VO$_2$max** is divided by the weight and is expressed in ml./min/kilogram. This is the relative capacity of oxygen intake. High **VO$_2$max** indicates a large capacity to oxidize energy supplies (carbohydrates and fatty acids). This is of course favorable to making long-term efforts. The measuring of the maximum capacity of oxygen intake is rather time-consuming and provides no absolute value judgment concerning the aerobic capacity of the cyclist. However, it is common belief that **VO$_2$max** of 60ml/min.kg is a base requirement to achieve good results as a cyclist.

The aerobic endurance training can be subdivided into three levels:
Aerobic Endurance Training level 1 (AET1), Aerobic Endurance Training level 2 (AET2) and Aerobic Endurance Training level 3 (AET3)

- **AET1**, also known as Long Slow Distance (LSD), is very important for a cyclist. These are training sessions which last a very long time, generally longer than a race. The pace is relatively low, so that you can easily chat during training. Energy is mainly provided by oxidation of fatty acids.

- In **AET2** as well, the training pace remains relatively low, but nevertheless higher than in the LSD. Although oxidation of fatty acids is still essential for energy supply, the share of oxidation of carbohydrates increases. By means of this type of training the cyclist prepares himself for the more intensive training coming.

  AET1 and AET2 sessions are very important because they will allow the cyclist to cycle at a higher pace on the basis of his fat metabolism, without addressing the carbohydrate store. This means that a cyclist having developed good aerobic endurance can more easily save his carbohydrate store during the race than a less well -trained cyclist can. A cyclist must not only pay attention to these training sessions during the preparation period, but also during the race season in between the tough races.

  During the first 6 weeks of the preparation period almost 100% of the training sessions besides the strength training must be spent on submaximal work.On an annual basis this percentage fluctuates between 75 and 80%.

- **AET3** sessions are shorter than the AET1 and AET2 sessions and the intensity is significantly higher. The cyclist has a less comfortable feeling, breathing rhythm goes quicker and talking becomes more difficult.

  This training takes place in the area under the threshold (see next page), and has a positive influence on the carbohydrate metabolism. By means of these high intensity endurance training sessions, the endurance limit is being moved, i.e. that you can cycle at a higher speed for a longer time.

  As the race season approaches the AET3 sessions will gain importance. This type of training is done from 4 to 6 weeks before the beginning of the competition, and can never account for more than 10 to 15% of the total training volume. A professional cyclist starts these training sessions in late December, an amateur later.

Threshold training

Threshold training refers to training sessions which are carried out at the threshold, using repetitions of approximately 5 to 15 minutes. These are intensive training sessions which especially have a favorable influence on the oxidation of carbohydrates as the energy source in the body. You should distinguish the threshold training on a flat track from threshold training uphill. On a flat track the intensity of these training sessions is just below and on the threshold. On an inclined track the training heart rate can be somewhat higher (therefore above the threshold) because when cycling uphill more muscle groups cooperate actively in making the effort.

Submaximal interval training

In the submaximal (or extensive) interval training, the training load is systematically varied with (active) recuperation. The intensity of the training is above the threshold, but remains submaximal. The duration of the strain amounts to 30 seconds to 5 minutes, the number of repetitions is rather high and the recovering time between the efforts is short.

High intensity interval training

High intensity (or intensive) interval training is the perfect means to train for **anaerobic endurance capacity**. For anaerobic endurance, the energy required is provided without mediation of oxygen. Energy is released by the breakdown of adenosine-triphosphate (ATP), creatine phosphate (CP) and glycogen which has been stored up in the muscles. This energy is immediately available, but also very rapidly consumed.

An additional disadvantage is that the breakdown of these energy stocks is paired with the piling-up of lactic acid (expressed in mmol/liter blood) in the muscles. Lactic acid is thus a waste product that blocks the muscular system. Piling-up lactic acid forces the cyclist to reduce the effort intensity drastically and to give the body time to remove the lactic acid. High intensity interval training actually teaches the body to cope with this lactic acid so that its piling-up is better endured. The anaerobic endurance capacity is therefore very important for efforts of high intensity and of short duration (for example at breakaways, fast closing of a gap, accelerations while cycling uphill etc.).

This base characteristic is best trained by doing successive short-term efforts (30 sec to 1 min 30 sec) at a very high, even maximum intensity. The number of repetitions is low (3 to 5 times) and the pause between the successive efforts is incomplete, so that the lactic acid has not been removed entirely when the next effort is started upon. These are very hard training sessions, which demand much from the cyclist.

Also important to know is that these training sessions, if being done too often, have a negative influence on the aerobic endurance capacity. Therefore it is absolutely inadvisable to do these training sessions during the first 4 to 6 weeks of the preparation period, when the primordial objective is the intensification of the aerobic endurance. It is even advisable to start just two to three weeks before the race season with these training sessions. For a professional cyclist this therefore means late January, for an amateur only late February. The share of these training sessions in the total training program is restricted up to 2 to 5% of the total training volume.

Note: the threshold

The term threshold causes quite a lot of confusion. The term threshold implies the heart rate which borders between the aerobic energy supplies and the anaerobic energy supplies. Threshold training means training in aerobic-anaerobic area. These training sessions are very effective to extend stamina, i.e. being able to perform without "going into the red".

The threshold must not be confused with maximum lactate steady-state. Maximum lactate steady-state refers to the maximum effort intensity which can be endured without observing an increase of the lactic acid quantity in blood during this effort.

Determining the individual training intensity for the different types of training

The first two weeks of the preparation period (week 3 and 4 of November) serve as a trial period stipulating the training workload for the strength training, starting this strength training and adapting the muscles to the cycling movement. In order to control training optimally it is high time to determine the individual training intensity for the different types of training in early December. Training within the right target heart rate will maximize the ability to perform.

This can be determined rather easily by means of the formula of Karvonen which is based on the resting heart rate and the maximum heart rate, or more sophisticated, but thus more precise, by means of stipulating the concentration of lactic acid during a test on the bicycle ergometer.

The formula of Karvonen

The heart rate during the effort generally provides a precise idea concerning the training intensity and the kind of the effort provided by the cyclist. Until a certain level, the heart rate increases linearly to the rising effort intensity. One should, however, take into account that apart from the effort of the body other factors can also influence the heart rate (lowering or raising). These factors will be further elaborated. The heart rate during the effort can also indicate the evolution of the cyclist's condition. When the cyclist notices that after a while he can achieve the same performance at a lower heart rate, he could conclude that his condition has improved.

The heart rate can be registered in several ways. In the first place. manually by feeling and counting the pulsation in the area of the heart, the carotid artery or the radial artery. This method is easy to handle when recording the resting heart rate, but very inaccurate when the heart rate needs to be counted immediately after an effort. Counting the heart rate during the effort is entirely impossible. The registration of the heart rate can be much more precise by means of the wireless heart rate monitors which have been common practice among cyclists for many years now. These heart rate monitors allow the cyclist to remain continuously informed on his heart rate during the effort.

In order to calculate the formula of Karvonen the cyclist needs to know his resting heart rate (RHR) and his maximum heart rate (HRM) very accurately.

The resting heart rate

The resting heart rate is best registered in the morning, some minutes after awaking. The circumstances in which this registration is done must always be the same, preferably lying down.

The maximum heart rate

The maximum heart rate is the heart rate which can be reached during a maximum effort, for example after a sprint uphill. Registering the maximum heart rate must be preceded by a sound warming-up, doing some accelerations in climax form towards the end of this warming-up. This means that during acceleration the pace is raised progressively. Warming-up must however not be too intensive, because the maximum heart rate can only be reached if the cyclist is not tired.

During a stage race a cyclist will actually notice that after some days it is no longer possible to reach the same high heart rate as during the beginning of the stage race. When a cyclist feels during training that he can no longer raise his heart rate, it may be time to scale back the training.

The maximum heart rate is therefore not due to training in itself, but to fatigue which successive training sessions bring along. The maximum heart rate never indicates the performance capacity of the cyclist. A cyclist with a high maximum heart rate has no more or no fewer capacities than a cyclist with a low maximum heart rate. The maximum heart rate decreases, however, when aging.

If the resting heart rate and the maximum heart rate are known, the training intensity can be calculated according to the formula of Karvonen. The training intensity is then expressed in percentage of the maximum effort capacity.

% (HRM–RHR) + RHR = HR during effort

For example

A cyclist having a resting heart rate of 52, and a maximum heart rate of 200, wants to train to 70% of his maximum effort capacity. His training heart rate is then calculated as follows:

$$0.7 \, (200-52) + 52 = 156$$

As the cyclist's condition improves, the resting heart rate drops and the training heart rate also decreases. If the cyclist in the example above has a resting heart rate 40, then his training heart rate to 70% of his maximum effort capacity will also be approximately 5 beats lower.

The training intensity for the different types of training, based on the formula of Karvonen, can be calculated as follows:

Nature of the training	% of the maximum effort capacity
recovery training	- 60%
Aerobic endurance training level 1 (AET1)	61-64%
Aerobic endurance training level 1 (AET2)	65-70%
Aerobic endurance training level 1 (AET3)	71-78%
Threshold training flat	79-81%
Threshold training uphill	82-84%
Submaximal interval training	85-89%
High intensity interval training	+ 90%

Elaborated example for a cyclist having a maximum heart rate of 200 and a resting heart rate of 40:

Nature of the training	training heart rate
Recovery training	- 136
Aerobic endurance training level 1 (AET1)	137-144
Aerobic endurance training level 1 (AET2)	145-152
Aerobic endurance training level 1 (AET3)	153-165
Threshold training flat	166-170
Threshold training uphill	171-175
Submaximal interval training	176-183
High intensity interval training	184+

Note:

You should however take into account that the heart rate is due to a number of factors apart from training:

- **Temperature and humidity degree**
  In warm weather and high air humidity, the heart rate increases, both in rest and during efforts. Between 16° C/61° F and 20° C/68° F the heart rate reaches its most normal values. As it grows colder it becomes more difficult to reach the heart rate limits for the different types of training. From 12° C/54° F, the heart rate limits can be reduced by one pulsation per degree.
  In temperatures above 25° C/77° F the heart rate increases more rapidly than usually. The high temperature forms an extra strain for the body. Therefore it is better to respect the heart rate indicated and therefore lower the pace.

- **Loss of fluids**
  Loss of fluids increases the heart rate during effort. It is thus very important to drink sufficiently during the training sessions and the races. It is wrong to think that drinking a lot is only necessary in warm and wet weather. Under colder circumstances as well, drinking regularly is a must.

- **Food**
  Eating food full of carbohydrates before, and drinking energy drinks during, the training and the race leads to a lower heart rate during the race. Someone who neglects to complete his carbohydrates store after high intensity training sessions and after races will no longer be able to obtain a high heart rate after a while. This will lead to being overtrained.

- **Refrigeration**
  Refrigeration during a long-term effort brings along a drop in the heart rate. Especially in warm and wet circumstances, refrigeration is absolutely necessary in order to keep the body temperature sufficiently low. If the body temperature rises too strongly this can lead to coordination impairments and later to heat coma. In extreme circumstances this overheating of the body may have fatal impact.

- **Illness**
An athlete who is ill has, both during rest and during effort, a (much) higher heart rate than usual. A sick body is not trainable. One of the causes of sudden death in sports is myocarditis, an inflammation of the myocardium.

  This disorder can arise during a viral infection (influenza) because the virus sticks to the myocardium. When ill, and even more so when the illness is accompanied by fever, one must never train.

- **Medicine**
Some medicine has a clear impact on the heart rate. If medicine must be taken, it is advisable to ask the doctor if training is permitted or not.

- **The muscle mass used**
Using more muscle mass during the effort increases heart rate. Therefore the heart rate in threshold training uphill is higher than on a flat track. During cycling uphill the arms and the torso are used more thoroughly than during cycling on a flat road.

- **Stress**
During a race the heart rate is, especially for cyclists prone to stress, higher than usual. For these athletes it is thus not very useful to have a heart rate monitor during races. For these cyclists it does not make sense to register the morning heart rate on the morning of a race.

- **Overtraining**
A cyclist who is over-trained can no longer reach the maximum heart frequency. The heart rate during effort is thus lower than usual. Sometimes this is wrongfully interpreted as a positive sign (a lower heart rate for the same effort).

Under limit heart rate AET3

Hr/Hm	205	200	195	190	185	180	175	170
35	154	151	147	144	140	137	133	130
40	156	152	149	145	142	138	135	131
45	157	154	150	147	143	140	136	133
50	159	155	152	148	145	141	138	134
55	160	157	153	150	146	143	139	136
60	162	158	155	151	148	144	141	137
65	163	160	156	153	149	146	142	139
70	165	161	158	154	151	147	144	140
75	166	163	159	156	152	149	145	142
80	168	164	161	157	154	150	147	143

Upper limit heart rate AET3

Hr/Hm	205	200	195	190	185	180	175	170
35	168	164	160	156	152	148	144	140
40	169	165	161	157	153	149	145	141
45	170	166	162	158	154	150	146	143
50	171	167	163	159	155	151	148	144
55	172	168	164	160	156	153	149	145
60	173	169	165	161	158	154	150	146
65	174	170	166	163	159	155	151	147
70	175	171	168	164	160	156	152	148
75	176	173	169	165	161	157	153	149
80	178	174	170	166	162	158	154	150

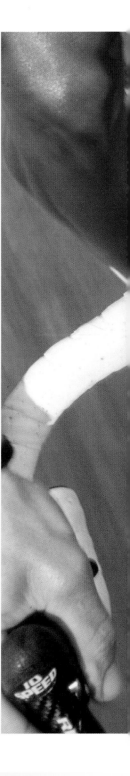

Under limit heart rate "threshold training on flat road"

Hr/Hm	205	200	195	190	185	180	175	170
35	168	164	160	156	152	148	144	140
40	169	165	161	157	153	149	145	141
45	170	166	162	158	154	150	146	143
50	171	167	163	159	155	151	148	144
55	172	168	164	160	156	153	149	145
60	173	169	165	161	158	154	150	146
65	174	170	166	163	159	155	151	147
70	175	171	168	164	160	156	152	148
75	176	173	169	165	161	157	153	149
80	178	174	170	166	162	158	154	150

Upper limit heart rate "threshold training on flat road"

Hr/Hm	205	200	195	190	185	180	175	170
35	173	169	165	161	157	152	148	144
40	174	170	166	162	157	153	149	145
45	175	171	167	162	158	154	150	146
50	176	172	167	163	159	155	151	147
55	177	172	168	164	160	156	152	148
60	177	173	169	165	161	157	153	149
65	178	174	170	166	162	158	154	150
70	179	175	171	167	163	159	155	151
75	180	176	172	168	164	160	156	152
80	181	177	173	169	165	161	157	153

Under limit heart rate "threshold training uphill"

Hr/Hm	205	200	195	190	185	180	175	170
35	173	169	165	161	157	152	148	144
40	174	170	166	162	157	153	149	145
45	175	171	167	162	158	154	150	146
50	176	172	167	163	159	155	151	147
55	177	172	168	164	160	156	152	148
60	177	173	169	165	161	157	153	149
65	178	174	170	166	162	158	154	150
70	179	175	171	167	163	159	155	151
75	180	176	172	168	164	160	156	152
80	181	177	173	169	165	161	157	153

Upper limit heart rates "threshold training uphill"

Hr/Hm	205	200	195	190	185	180	175	170
35	178	174	169	165	161	157	153	148
40	179	174	170	166	162	158	153	149
45	179	175	171	167	163	158	154	150
50	180	176	172	168	163	159	155	151
55	181	177	173	168	164	160	156	152
60	182	178	173	169	165	161	157	152
65	183	178	174	170	166	162	157	153
70	183	179	175	171	167	162	158	154
75	184	180	176	172	167	163	159	155
80	185	181	177	172	168	164	160	156

Under limit heart rates "submaximal interval training"

Hr/Hm	205	200	195	190	185	180	175	170
35	178	174	169	165	161	157	153	148
40	179	174	170	166	162	158	153	149
45	179	175	171	167	163	158	154	150
50	180	176	172	168	163	159	155	151
55	181	177	173	168	164	160	156	152
60	182	178	173	169	165	161	157	152
65	183	178	174	170	166	162	157	153
70	183	179	175	171	167	162	158	154
75	184	180	176	172	167	163	159	155
80	185	181	177	172	168	164	160	156

Upper limit heart rates "submaximal interval training"

Hr/Hm	205	200	195	190	185	180	175	170
35	186	182	177	173	169	164	160	155
40	187	182	178	174	169	165	160	156
45	187	183	179	174	170	165	161	156
50	188	184	179	175	170	166	161	157
55	189	184	180	175	171	166	162	157
60	189	185	180	176	171	167	162	158
65	190	185	181	176	172	167	163	158
70	190	186	181	177	172	168	163	159
75	191	186	182	177	173	168	164	160
80	191	187	182	178	173	169	165	160

The lactic acid test

In rest the lactic acid concentration in the blood amounts to 1 to 2 mmol/liter. This lactic acid concentration remains constant as long as the cyclist remains in rest or trains to a moderate intensity. As long as the lactic acid concentration remains stable or only increases slightly, the effort can be continued for a very long time, theoretically speaking, because the lactic acid formed is being removed during the effort itself. When the effort intensity continues to increase, the lactic acid will however also start to increase in a first stage. As the intensity continues to increase, the lactic acid concentration also starts rising more considerably, and at high intensity will eventually show a very strong increase curve. At this moment the cyclist will be obliged to stop the effort or to strongly scale back the intensity. For a well-trained cyclist the cycling speed will be higher before the curve shows a strong increase than for a less well-trained cyclist.

By means of laboratory tests, a very precise link can be determined between the lactic acid concentration and the capacity which the cyclist provides, and between the acid concentration and the heart rate.

This is generally tested using a gradual effort test on a bicycle ergometer. The time span of one effort stage should take at least 4 minutes because only after this period a constant lactic acid value will be reached.

The training recommendation is based on the course of the lactic acid curve:

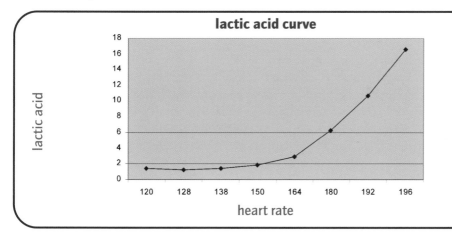

The point where the lactic acid curve shows a strong increase (heart rate 164) is vital. We can conclude that the threshold is situated here.

Training sessions December

As soon as the training heart rate ranges for the different training forms are stipulated, the training sessions can be controlled much more thoroughly.
For December, the following objectives are postulated:

- The training volume is gradually forced up within the heart rate ranges for **AET1 and AET2 sessions**. The cyclist continues to train at low gear ratio, in which is strived for 100-105 rotations/minute.

- A part of these training sessions is still carried out with **fixed gear**.

- To prevent the cyclist fossilizing in this relatively slow tempo, there are from time to time short and violent accelerations in the beginning of the aerobic endurance training sessions. These are called **anaerobic stimulation training sessions** which are meant to stimulate the anaîrobic capacity of the cyclist.

  An example of an endurance training session lasting 3 hours:
  - 20 min easy riding
  - 5x30 sec high tempo, rec. in between 3 min easy riding
  - easy endurance training, level AET1–AET2, low gear ratio (suppleness)

  It has been quite some time now since the cyclist has addressed his anaerobic energy supplies. It is thus not astonishing that these rhythm changes during the first training sessions are experienced as rather tough. As these training sessions are done more often, they will also be more fluent.

- Late December a professional cyclist must be able to cycle 5 hours without problems. He must also strive for a week volume of 600 km. because he must be ready to leave in January for a training trip in which the training volume must still be forced up considerably. By late December it is also advisable for professional cyclists to already do some **block-system training sessions,** i.e. training sessions in which you ride during a short time close to the threshold (threshold training flat road).

  An amateur on the other hand strives in late December to aerobic endurance training sessions of 4 hours in length, and to a week volume of 400 km. Block-system training sessions are not yet necessary for him, since the competitive season usually only starts early March.

- The **strength training** as well evolves normally, both in the gym and on the bicycle. The professional cyclists and the amateurs strive both for a proportion of 2 specific strength training sessions-2 strength training sessions in the gym.

  For the specific strength training it is very important that the threshold is not exceeded. This training must not be an anaerobic training session.
  A professional cyclist, who–normally speaking–starts the competition in the beginning of February, stops strength training in the gym by late December. An amateur on the other hand, who only starts the competition in March, still trains a month longer in the gym.

The fourth week functions as a recovery week. At the end of this week there is time for a test.

This cycle is best integrated when the cyclist already has a sufficient training base, on the one hand to be able to control a large training volume during the first week of the cycle, on the other hand to be able to put enough intensity in the training during the second and the third week.

A last cycle is the **thrust cycle**.

In this cycle an intensive week is varied with a relatively easy week. Since you train very hard both quantitatively and qualitatively during the intensive week you should make sure not to reach overload.

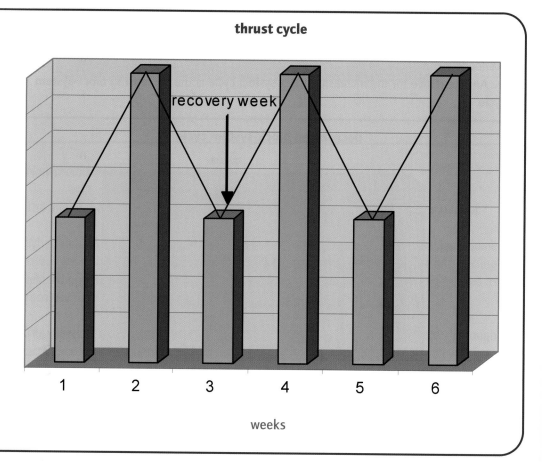

thrust cycle

recovery week

weeks

CHAPTER 3

1 JANUARY–31 JANUARY

From this moment on the training sessions of professional cyclists and amateurs clearly begin to differ.

The professional cyclists are only 4 weeks away from the start of the new competitive season, and the training sessions must be more and more competitive now, although the competitive objectives partly determine the training workload.

Professional cyclists

We suppose that the cyclists need to reach their top level during the classic springtime races.

Roughly the next 4 weeks are divided into 2 periods:

Period 1: emphasis on:
- Specific strength training on the road (uphill)
- Aerobic endurance training sessions level 2 (training volume)
- Aerobic endurance training sessions level 3
- Threshold training
- Anaerobic stimulation training

Period 2: emphasis on:
- Specific strength training on the road (uphill)
- Aerobic endurance training sessions level 2 (training volume)
- Aerobic endurance training sessions level 3
- Threshold training
- Anaerobic training sessions (competitive), without exaggerating however.

Period 1

It is advisable to leave on a training trip (for about 10 days) to a hilly area where the weather circumstances are fine early January. This way you can ensure the training continuity, and the uphill strength and threshold training can be done better.

			suppleness (under threshold)–10 min at threshold, approximately 80 rot./min. –5 min suppleness under threshold • In between the climbs: suppleness
Friday	1	Aerobic endurance training	5-6 hours long endurance training with tempo changes • Level AET1–AET3, min. 90-100 rot./min. During the training accelerating some times progressively: 2x (30 min AET1– 30 min AET2.- 20 min AET3) • If possible, last 2 hours behind the motorcycle.
Saturday	1	Recovery	90 min easy riding, level recovery training
Sunday	1	Threshold training	5 hours training on hilly track • Slope of approximately 20 min in length Totally 4 times this slope. • 1° slope: suppleness, 90 rot./min., at threshold • 2° slope: alternating 5 min suppleness - 5 min strength 40-60 rot./min., never above threshold • 3° slope: 80 rot./min., some beats above threshold. • 4° slope: alternating 5 min suppleness - 5 min specific strength 40-60 rot./min., never above threshold • In between cycling uphill suppleness • Rest of the training session: suppleness, if possible last 11/2 hour behind the motorcycle

TOTAL approximately 900 km

After the first period some recovery days must be planned.

It would not be inadvisable to leave for another training location for the second period in order to avoid monotony.

A training week for these cyclists could look like this

Day		Training Type	Description
Monday	1	Strength	Specific strength training on rollers • Never above threshold • Cooling down for a sufficiently long time
Tuesday	1	Suppleness	120 min suppleness • Fixed gear • AET2
Wednesday	1	Aerobic endurance training	210 min aerobic endurance training • AET1-AET2 • + 90 rot./min. • after 30 min warming-up 8x10 sec sprint; rec. 1 min easy riding
Thursday	1	Strength	Specific strength training on rollers. • Never above threshold.
Friday	1	Anaerobic pivot training	Anaerobic pivot training on rollers: • 20 min easy riding • 6 x 30 sec high tempo, in between 2 min easy riding • 30 min easy riding
Saturday	1	Aerobic endurance training Suppleness	150 min aerobic endurance training • Fixed gear • AET1-AET2
Sunday	1	Threshold training	240 min on a hilly track • Uphill till threshold

CHAPTER 4

1 FEBRUARY–28 FEBRUARY

Professional cyclists

For most professional cyclists, the actual competitive season starts now. During this month a lot of stage races are planned. Real training is not done often, because of the overloading race scheme. The periods between the races are needed to recover. Easy endurance training sessions, preferably partly behind the motorcycle, are advisable in this period.

Amateurs

The training priorities of the amateurs during this period are similar to those of the professional cyclists in January. The best-structured amateur teams also leave on a training trip, albeit only once, for two weeks.

The training priorities during this period are:

- Forcing up the training volume

- Threshold training

- Race-specific training

- Maintenance of the suppleness training sessions

- Specific strength training (the general strength training is from now on crossed out from the training program)

Wednesday 1	Aerobic endurance training	4 hours long endurance training • AET1	
Thursday 1	Recovery	60 min easy riding or complete rest day	
Friday 1	Race-specific training	300 min: • 30 min easy riding • 10x breakaway 30 sec at full speed, rec. 3 min easy riding • 15 min easy riding • "Turning around" in small groups (6 cyclists), after 2 min changing, everyone does 6 relays in total • Further varied training on hilly track with breakaways on the slopes	
Saturday 1	Aerobic endurance training	4 hours long endurance training • Easy endurance training in group, AET1-2	
Sunday 1	Recovery	90 min easy riding, level recovery	

Cyclists who feel tired should plan a recovery day in time. Some important indications meaning you have to plan an extra day recovering are: feeling tired, a higher resting heart rate and no longer being able to force up the heart rate during the effort.

It is also very important that the cyclist respects the type of the training. It does not make sense to always want to train with daggers drawn and then return completely fatigued from the training trip. This risk is not imaginary at all when you train in-group during a certain period. Frequently one cyclist does not want to be inferior to the other one during training, and the individual training intensities are not respected anymore. These cyclists rapidly have to pay the price after the training period, by suffering a condition loss instead of gaining a condition profit.

After such a training period it is also necessary to plan a recovery period lasting from some days up to a week. Afterwards the cyclist is undoubtedly ready to start his first race.

CHAPTER 6

TRAINING SESSIONS FOR YOUNGSTERS AND JUNIORS

So far training sessions for amateurs and professional cyclists have been dealt with. Obviously this kind of training is not intended for elementary and intermediate levels. Although some basic principles still apply.

Youngsters

Quite often you can establish that the top notch among the youngsters quickly disappears as soon as they enter an older category. Among juniors they can still keep up appearances, but becoming amateur quite often means the end of performances of a high level.

The explanation for this phenomenon can generally be found in the fact that in young people there is often a difference between chronological and biological age. The biological age is the age based on the biological development of the body. One 15-year-old may have the physical development of a 17-year-old, whereas his peer standing at the same start line has a biological development of a 13-year-old. In reality there is thus an age difference of four years.

Therefore it is not at all hard to guess which cyclist will have obtained most victories at the end of the season. One look at the stand of a youngster race often tells the whole story. Frequently the strapping lads are on the highest position. Around age 18 the difference in physical development has been leveled out, and other factors, like training and talent, are responsible for the performance level.

Among newcomers there is thus a big difference in physical development. This difference influences the training approach of this youth category. You have to take the physical development of the cyclist into account.

CHAPTER 7

TRAINING FOR CYCLING TOURISTS

Cycling training is not only there for competitive cyclists. Next to this group there are quite a lot of cycling tourists who are very fanatically involved in their sport, without wanting to explicitly compare themselves with others. Their performances are nevertheless worth some attention as well.

Just consider for instance the classic races for cycling tourists. These concern rides that often account for more than 200 km, most of the time passing the same difficulties that the professionals must conquer. Moreover there are, especially in France and Italy splendidly planned routes that go to the top of the great cycling tours.

An example is the Marmotte (190 km), involving climbs of the Croix de Fer (out of category), the Telegraphe (2nd category), the Galibier (out of category) and to top it all the arrival on L' Alpe d'Huez (out of category).

Here you can, aiming at the finishing time, fight for a gold, silver or bronze medal, and even for some glory between kindred spirits. The preparation on these "randonnées" often is so intense that you can begin to put some questions marks after the term "cycling tourist". These cycling fanatics train very hard to reach their personal goals, even to that degree that most of the basic principles applying to amateurs and even to professional cyclists, also apply to them.

The Winter period (December–March)

We start from the fact that this group of cycling tourists has a normal professional life, and that they can most of the time train decently during weekends. A large part of the training sessions will be done on rollers, due to the cold and wet weather conditions, and the total training volume is obviously much lower than for amateurs and professionals.

But if during the summer months you want to shine in the tours mentioned above, you cannot neglect cycling training during winter. Preferably you put some specific accents.

The stresses during the winter period are:

- Suppleness training
- Strength training, especially specific. Those who have much spare time can also do general strength training in the gym, while adopting the same method as mentioned before.
- Gradually forcing up the training volume

Suppleness training

Suppleness training can best be done on rollers. Twice 30 to 40 minutes a week are enough during this period. You cycle at more than 100 rotations per minute, regularly even at 120 rotations per minute. An aid to break the monotony is to cycle while the radio or Cd-player is on, and in turn slightly forcing up the intensity during a song and when the next song starts lowering the intensity again, or in turn cycling at a higher or lower number of rotations per minute.

The heart rate during these training sessions must always remain in the zone AET1-AET2, including once in a while some peaks into the zone AET3.

Strength training

If due to lack of time you have to choose between general and specific strength training, the specific strength training should absolutely be preferred. It is indeed important to train as specific as possible. General strength training is only useful if supplementing the specific training sessions.

You can do this kind of training adopting the method mentioned above:

- Number of rot./min: 40 to 60
- Intensity: always below threshold
- Set-up of 4 x 1min to 8 x 3 min in a period of 9 weeks.
- Number of training sessions a week: one, if possible two.

If opting for general strength training the principles already described still apply. The stress is on the development of strength endurance capacity. Therefore you work with 40 to 50 % of 1 RM, and you gradually force up from 3 x 10 repetitions till 5 x 20 repetitions. Preferably you also train two times a week.

Forcing up training volume

Especially during weekends you can find some time to build up a certain training volume. In a first phase (till late January) one aerobic endurance training session during the weekend is enough. The volume is forced up gradually from 2 to 4 hours. Emphasis is on suppleness training, the intensity remains relatively low (heart rate in the zone AET1-AET2.) Most of the time you cycle in a group. Cold and wet weather conditions often make it difficult to regularly train on the road.

An alternative you can find in the so-called tour routes for mountain bikes. These involve tours of about 40 km on frequently sandy or muddy and bumpy track. Because your speed is much lower than on the road there is less cooling down. Such tour routes therefore are during winter often a lot more pleasant than long training sessions on the road. Danger however rises in the intensity. You most of the time cycle to a much higher heart rate than during road training sessions. Experience teaches us that cycling sportsmen ride "into the red" during the main part of the tour. Such training sessions are thus not appropriate to force up aerobic endurance capacity. Checking the heart rate during the effort can however be the solution to this problem.

From February onwards you can if the weather allows it plan a second endurance training session during the weekend.

From now on you can also introduce some anaerobic stimulations during one of the endurance sessions. This means that after a thorough warming-up you ride at full speed for 20 to 30 sec. In the beginning phase the number of repetitions is small (two to three). Afterwards this can be forced up to about six repetitions.

Of course you must make sure not to train as hard every week, or you should mind to force up training labor week after week. You need to pay enough attention to recovery. Therefore it is not bad to once in a while, after a tough week of training, scale back training significantly. Training only ensures profit after enough recovery.

Next to these enthusiastic, almost competitive cycling tourists there is also the category of cycling tourists who cycle out of medical concerns in order to acquire a good basic condition. They are less fanatically involved in their sport, which they take up as soon as wheather conditions are more pleasant.

Nevertheless it is also important for them to remain more or less active on the bicycle during the winter months. About three times a week cycling on rollers during 30 to 45 min should be enough. If the weather allows it, you can of course also cycle outside, possibly on the mountain bike. In this case as well the principle that mountain biking is generally too intense applies, especially for cycling tourists who are not often on their bicycles during the winter period. Doing sports out of medical concerns requires almost exclusively aerobic efforts.

This means that the cycling intensity must be relatively low almost all the time, and the training progression is in the fact that training volume is forced up. In other words you should make sure to particularly cycle in the zone AET1-AET2, having now and then peaks into the zone AET3. All intensity that is higher misses the eventual goal.

The risk for these cycling tourists is now particularly in the fact that the group with whom they cycle is generally heterogeneous concerning age and performance level. In order not to be forced to needless and possibly less healthy efforts, it is really advisable to always cycle with cyclists of the same level.

Groups of cycling tourists therefore should subdivide into two groups, in which one of these groups is restricted for cycling tourists of a lower level, or for those who have, for whatever reason, a training deprivation. It is also crystal clear that a heart rate monitor can be not only for the competitive cyclist, but also for the ordinary cycling tourist, an especially useful aid.

CHAPTER 8

SPECIFIC TRAINING SESSIONS

Time trial training

Time trialing is a very difficult and mentally straining discipline which demands the utmost of the cyclist. During this stage of the race the cyclist can seldom compare the energy he has to provide with the energy of his opponents, apart from the fact that he sometimes is informed on the interim results of his direct competitors. His only point of reference consists mainly of his own experience which teaches him which tempo he can adopt during a time trial.

Technical approach

Lance Armstrong rode a time trial in the Tour de France 2000 of more than 50 km to an average speed of 54 km/hour. This performance is characteristic of the evolution that speed during time trialing has undergone lately.

The reason for this cannot only be found in the perfected training methods and the better medical support, but also in the evolution in material (bicycle and attire) and position on the bicycle.

Time trialing is a technical discipline, in which you must try and do all that is possible to overcome a number of opposing forces. The choice of the material, the bicycle attire and the position on the bicycle are vitally important to overcome these forces which are: the friction caused by pedals, pedal bracket, chain and derailleur; the rolling resistance; the air resistance and gravity force.

1. **The friction caused by pedals, pedal bracket, chain and derailleur**

This resistance is, in high-quality, well maintained bicycles , very low.

2. **The rolling resistance**

The rolling resistance depends on a number of factors:

- Width of the racing tires: broad tires give more rolling resistance than narrow tires.
- Pressure in the tires: one could state that the more pressure one can put in the tire the less rolling resistance there will be. However a slight dent in the tire must still remain possible.

CHAPTER 9

TRAINING AND OVERTRAINING

What is overtraining?

Cyclists seldom or never train too little. Results often disappoint anyway. For a lot of cyclists this is the signal to train even harder without there being much improvement. On the contrary performances will often decline still further. How is that possible? To answer this question we need to analyze the term **training**.

Training is administering systematic physical stimulations to the body, taking into account the capacity of the body. These stimulations bring about changes in the body which lead, when considering the correct proportion effort–recovery, to an increase of the performance capacity.

In this definition there are some important data:

Taking into account the capacity of the body
Every cyclist has a certain training capacity. This capacity is not always consistent. Insufficient sleep, bad nutrition, illness or stress, for instance, can reduce the capacity of the body. Not every cyclist has the same capacity. Some cyclists can perform more training labor than others.

Therefore it makes no sense to just copy training diagrams of good cyclists. It is far more important to take into account the training principles applied by good cyclists, and apply these principles considering your own capacity. Moreover it is not so that the cyclist with the largest capacity by definition also obtains the best results. Some cyclists can achieve better results with a lower training tax than cyclists who train harder and more frequently.

If the training stimuli are stronger than the individual capacity, the cyclist will be over-trained after a while. You can distinguish between *qualitative overtraining* and *quantitative overtraining*. The cause for qualitative overtraining needs to be looked for in the intensity of the training stimuli, i.e. you cycle too fast (intensively) during training. In quantitative overtraining on the other hand the training volume is too large. Not the intensity, but the training duration is too long. Overtraining often appears as a combination of these two forms of overtraining.

CHAPTER 10

TRAINING APART FROM TRAINING

So far, a lot of aspects of cycling training have been taken into consideration. However these aspects do not stipulate the performance potential entirely. The performance is the eventual result of a lot of factors. Apart from training, these are talent, nutrition, material, insight in the race, medical support, mental strength, social environment, hygiene, team structure, nature of the track....

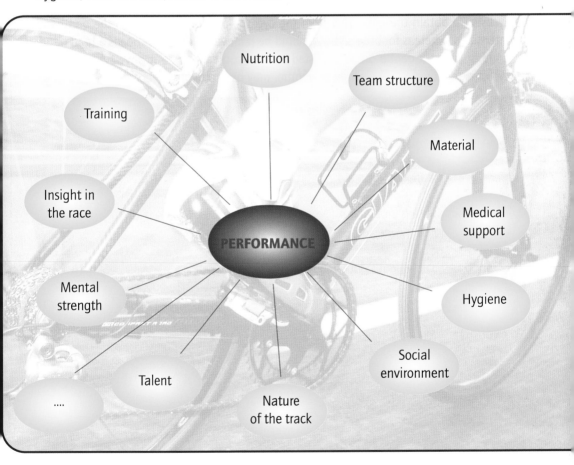

It is impossible to tell which of these factors is most important. The chain is but as strong as the weakest link. Supposedly this is the reason why there are so few great champions: it is very difficult to get all factors in a row at an optimal level. On average there is a weak point here and there.

Lifestyle

Apart from mental strength, the cyclist's lifestyle apart from training is largely contributory to a succeeding or failing cycling career. Especially for young cyclists it is important to get used to a disciplined way of life early on, paying close attention to training, nutrition and rest. Building out a cycling career is infinitely more than only training and riding races.

Frequently a young cyclist already decides at 18 years old to apply himself completely to cycling. This choice demands a lot of discipline from the cyclist still in the early preparation period. He has plenty of spare time besides training; and as a result he might stay in bed in the morning, go out with friends after training and go to bed late at night. Young people who choose a cycling career must follow a fixed pattern in which they get up early in the morning, have breakfast, leave for training in time, pay attention to their training (filling in a training diary, a possible print of training heart rates,....), then rest after training and tend to the maintenance of their material the rest of the day.

Of course there is still time for other activities. These activities however cannot disturb the recovery and cannot prevent the cyclist from going to bed early. Someone who chooses cycling IS a cyclist, not only during training and races, but always, 24/7.

A cyclist who does not take care of himself has more chance than other cyclists of disturbing his training by banal colds which are the consequence of contact with certain viruses. One had better avoid colds by not coming into contact with these viruses.

This is however impossible because viruses are spread by sneezes, coughs and even by ordinary breathing. Especially when having a weakened immune system the cyclist is more liable to these viruses. Research has shown that moderate training sessions have a positive impact on the immune system, while intensive training sessions have a negative impact.

Schematically this can be presented as shown on the next page.

- **Ferritine**
Ferritine is a protein-iron complex which indicates the iron reserve in the body. Iron is needed for the production of RBC and hemoglobin. A shortage of iron decreases hemoglobin quality and the number of RBC.

- **Magnesium**
Magnesium plays an important role in energy metabolism. A shortage of magnesium manifests itself clinically by a disturbed nerve-muscle function (among other things cramps) and muscle weakness.

Altitude training

The parameters above show that the number of red blood cells plays an important role in the performance capacity of the cyclist.

The best natural means to multiply this number of RBC and hemoglobin is altitude training. This raised production is an adaptation phenomenon of the body which arises under the influence of the reduced atmospheric pressure.

The conditions for good altitude training are:

- Stay on more than 1500m
- A stay on altitude for at least 3 weeks

In practice an altitude training period must be subdivided into a number of phases:

- **Phase 1:** the acclimatization phase.
You should give the body time to adapt to altitude. On average this phase lasts 3 to 5 days. In the beginning of this phase there is a clearly raised rest pulse. The training volume and the training intensity must consciously be kept very low. Once the resting heart rate has reached its normal value, you can start the next phase.
- **Phase 2:**
This phase lasts approximately 5 days. Training is progressively intensified, with a clear emphasis on the training volume, and not on the training intensity. Therefore you only do extensive training sessions.
- **Phase 3:**
During the previous phases the body has gotten time to adapt optimally to altitude. From now on you can train intensively. Do not forget however that the body recovers more slowly from the effort on altitude. Moreso than at sea level, you should pay attention to the recovery phases.

When returning from altitude training some elementary rules must also be observed:

- The first 10 days after returning to sea level are necessary to adapt again to the new situation. During this phase the emphasis is on lighter, extensive training sessions. This phase is a supercompensation phase to maximally profit from the effects of the past altitude training.
- After these 10 days the cyclist reaches a stage of increased performance level. Especially during the third week after the return to sea level the cyclist could achieve top performances.

But not all studies univocally emphasize the positive impact of altitude training, because:

- The maximum heart rate decreases by 1% per 400m altitude
- The maximal oxygen uptake decreases by 10% per 1000m, starting to count from 1200m
- To reach the same performance as on sea level, more carbohydrates are consumed at altitude
- Speed with which lactic acid is removed has slowed down
- When training at altitude, recovery has slowed down
- By the fall of the plasma volume the increase of the number of RBC and hemoglobin is only relative
- The quality of the RBC has decreased
- Generally speaking the cyclist sleeps less well during an altitude training period
- The appetite diminishes in comparison with sea level
- At altitude there is a higher risk of dehydration

Sometimes you opt for other procedures to get round these disadvantages:

- Training at altitude and sleeping at sea level
- Training at sea level and sleeping at altitude
  Especially this last procedure is said to be most effective. The research results on this are however not certified (yet).

CHAPTER 11

THE NUTRITION OF THE CYCLIST

As mentioned above the cyclist's performance is determined by numerous factors. All these factors are very important to reach the individual maximal performance level. But for this reason the saying "the chain is as strong as the weakest link" is applicable to cycling more than any other sport. One of the weak links for cyclists is the nutrition pattern. It is indeed striking how few cyclists are informed on the correct dietary habits, and especially of the catastrophic impact of bad nutrition.

To improve our insight into the nutrition pattern of the cyclist we should ponder about the energy supplies of the body. The two large energy sources of the body are carbohydrates and fatty acids. In extreme circumstances protein can also be applied as an energy source. In this last case the muscles are, however, literally demolished. It is clear that this would lead to a loss of condition within a very short period.

When are fatty acids and when are carbohydrates applied as energy source? During efforts of very low intensity, almost exclusively fatty acids are applied as energy source. If the effort intensity increases, the share of carbohydrates will increase as an energy supplier, and even to the degree that during very intensive efforts energy is exclusively provided by oxidation of carbohydrates.

These carbohydrates have been piled up in the body under the form of glycogen in the muscles and in the liver. This carbohydrate store is limited. Generally it is believed that during very intense efforts the carbohydrate store is consumed after approximately 90 minutes. Research has shown that on average after intensive training sessions, only 5% of the muscle glycogen consumed while training is produced per hour. When muscle glycogen is completely exhausted, it takes 20 hours before the muscle glycogen stocks again reach a normal level.

The fatty acid store in the body on the other hand is seemingly inexhaustible. There are two disadvantages of the energy supply by oxidation of fatty acids in comparison with the oxidation of carbohydrates: first, this energy supply gets started more slowly, and second, for the same quantity oxygen uptake, less energy is provided by oxidation of fatty acids than by oxidation of carbohydrates. What are the consequences for the cyclist?

A cyclist of 70 kilograms consumes, without training, daily approximately 2700 Kcal. If this cyclist trains 3 to 4 hours calmly, then his usage rises to approximately 4000 Kcal. If he intensively trains 4-5 hours on a hilly track, then his usage can rise to 5000-6000 Kcal.

It is advisable to incorporate sufficient Kcal particularly at breakfast to provide the energy for coming training labor. It is also good to eat snacks, so the cyclist prevents a hungry feeling. In the evening, on the other hand, it is best to eat less.

As mentioned before, the quantity of carbohydrates which a cyclist must take daily depends on training labor provided. On average this need can be calculated as follows:

- during recovery days: 4 to 5 g CH/kilogram
- during average training days (3 to 4 hrs endurance training): 7 to 8 g CH/kilogram
- during tough training days (4 to 6 hrs intense training): 10-12 gr. CH/kilogram

A cyclist weighing 70 kilograms must take approximately 800gr carbohydrates during tough training days. During hard race days this can be even more!

Share of Kcal, protein, fats and carbohydrates of some common nutrients by 100 g				
	Kcal	Protein		Carbohydrates
Banana	88	1	0	20
Apple	50	0	0	12
Orange	47	1	0	11
Kiwi	40	1	0	9
Muesli without sugar	390	11	8	68
Muesli with sugar	396	11	11	64
Oat malt	363	13	7	62
Cornflakes	370	7	1	84
Muesli bar	440	5	17	67
Milk skimmed	37	4	0.1	5
Milk semi-skimmed	46	4	1.5	5
Milk whole	63	4	3.4	5
Yogurt skimmed	35	4	0.1	4
Yogurt semi-skimmed	49	4	1.5	5
Yogurt whole	85	5	4.5	6
Brown bread	248	10	3	45
Whole-wheat bread	222	9	3	41
Margarine	730	0	80	1
Cheese 20+	245	34	12	0
Cheese 50+	370	23	31	0
Ham, raw	199	23	12	0
Chicken roll	166	24	7	2
Chocolate sprinklings	431	6	17	64
Marmalade	112	0	0	28

Share of Kcal, protein, fats and carbohydrates of some common nutrients by 100 g			
	Kcal	Protein	Carbohydrates
Spaghetti raw	350	12	2	71
Spaghetti cooked	94	3	1	19
Pizza, cheese and tomato			
Rice unboiled	346	7	1	78
Rice cooked	147	3	0	33
Potato, cooked	76	2	0	17
Fries	310	5	15	38
Cauliflower, raw	14	2	0	2
Carrots, raw	11	1	0	2
Endive, raw	5	1	0	0
Peas, cooked	60	4	0	11
Raw vegetables	14	1	0	2
Tomatoes	11	1	0	2
Leek, raw	24	1	0	0
Vegetable soup	34	1	2	3
Cod fish, cooked	105	23	1	0
Salmon	271	28	18	0
Chicken filet	158	31	4	0
Turkey filet	158	31	4	0
Breakfast bacon	404	15	38	0
Pork tenderloin	147	28	4	0
Beefsteak	139	27	3	1
Roast beef	167	28	6	1
Pudding, vanilla	114	4	3	19
Ice	182	3	9	22

During a stage race it is not that simple to take the necessary kcal and carbohydrates. During a hard mountain stage the calorie usage can rise to 8000–9000 kcal. This energy can but does not have to be entirely replenished during the race, because the cyclist starts having a certain reserve. The cyclist must eat regularly during the race anyway, both solid food and (a lot of) energy drinks and thirst quenchers, and immediately after the arrival he has to start drinking energy drinks, during the first 30' at least 500 ml, during the next period 500 ml every 45', until 2 to 3 liters have been consumed. Later in the evening a meal having a high share of carbohydrates must be provided, also including protein.

Do protein supplements have to be taken?

Protein is the building material of the body. As mentioned before, they only are addressed as fuel of the body in extreme cases, viz. at complete and continuing exhaustion of the glycogen stocks.

In contrast to the intake of carbohydrates, you can assume that a normal nutrition pattern always contains sufficient protein. An endurance sportsman has a daily protein need of approximately 1.4 g/kilogram. A cyclist weighing 70 kilograms needs approximately 91 g protein per day. If you know that a piece of chicken weighing approximately 200 g already provides almost half of the daily amount, it should be clear that you do not have to strive for extra protein supplementing. Only at the beginning of a new training advancement and in periods of strength training should supplementing be considered.

What to do in case of overweight?

A lot of cyclists sometimes struggle during, and even after the winter period with being overweight. It is strictly dissuaded to reach your ideal weight by means of a strict diet. A too high negative energy balance (more energy is consumed than is taken in) leads after some time to reduction of the muscles (protein is used as energy supplier), prevents the recovery of the body and therefore leads to overtraining, bringing along a significant fall of the performance potential.

That is why some important pieces of advice are:

- Limit weight increase during the winter period. It makes no sense to eat without brakes during the preparation period. Stop at 2 to 3 kilograms above the ideal weight.
- In case of overweight, start early with an adapted nutrition pattern avoiding useless nutrition such as sweets and soda. If necessary you should strive for a **slightly** negative energy balance, so that the ideal weight can be reached very gradually. This slightly negative energy balance is only necessary when, in spite of the adapted nutrition pattern and increasing training labor, the body weight does not decrease. Maximum 2 kilograms per month seem a safe margin to lose weight.
- It is best for a cyclist to lose weight by means of long, relatively easy endurance training sessions. During these training sessions fatty acids are oxidized. Intensive training sessions mainly oxidize carbohydrates.
- When following a diet you must always pay enough attention to the fact that the diet is not at the expense of carbohydrates. Especially intensive training labor requires permanent replenishing the carbohydrates under all circumstances, irrespective of the fact that the cyclist must lose weight. For reasons mentioned above fat must keep its place in nutrition as well.

Over the last years the fixed idea has arisen that a cyclist only stands sharp if his body fat is reduced up to 6%. This is absolutely untrue, because the percentage body fat is very personal. Some cyclists have by nature a very low percentage body fat. For them it is not difficult to reach 6%. Other cyclists have by nature a much higher percentage body fat. They reach those 6% only after following a very strict diet, in which they always show a negative energy balance. They take too few carbohydrates, as a result of which the energy stocks in their muscles are no longer replenished after intense training. Moreover in the nutrition pattern of these cyclists, there is generally no room for fatty acids. The consequence often is a spectacular drop of their performance potential. Research has shown that too fast weight loss leads to reduction of the aerobic and anaerobic capacity, of absolute strength and of strength endurance.

Following a very strict diet therefore is, for most cyclists, catastrophic.

The ideal weight of a cyclist cannot be captured in a postulated weight or fat percentage. A cyclist knows from experience when he is "sharp", and which weight he must reach to achieve his best performance. If a cyclist trains well, and takes into account the elementary nutrition directives such as mentioned above, strict diets are not necessary.

How about nutrition supplements and other preparations?

Concerning nutrition supplements and preparations it is difficult to still see the forest for the trees. Some supplements however prove to be really effective:

- **Creatine:** is an amino acid which functions in a muscle developing way, and is advisable during strength training. Research has proven that creatine is only significant for explosive sport efforts. Endurance sportsmen such as cyclists profit (apart from strength training) little from using creatine.

- **Arginine:** is an amino acid which, when administered in sufficiently large quantities, stimulates the pituitary gland. Because of this the production of the human growth hormone is stimulated. The human growth hormone improves recovery after effort.

- **Ornitine:** an amino acid with the same functioning as arginine

- **Glutamine:** an amino acid which reduces muscle demolition and reinforces the immune system. It is interesting to use glutamine in combination with creatine.

- **Antioxidants:** in the body as a result of the metabolism and energy production free radicals are being produced. These free radicals are among other things responsible for cardiac diseases, some forms of cancers, aging and muscular ache after effort. Research has also shown that training increases the amount of free radicals. Antioxidants are substances which neutralize the damaging functioning of free radicals. Thus the damage to muscle cells would be less large for sportsmen who take supplementing antioxidants than for those who do not take these supplements.

- **Vitamins and mineral supplements:** very many cyclists take such supplements, and generally even in very large quantities. These supplements are necessary if too few fruits and vegetables are eaten. A cyclist who eats every day at least 5 pieces of fruit, and eats fresh vegetables, does not need these (expensive) preparations.

- **Vitamin C:** this vitamin nevertheless asks particular attention. On the one hand it belongs to the antioxidants, on the other hand it has been proved that vitamin C raises the resistance of the body against infections. A cyclist who trains intensely has an inferior resistance against infections, because due to the

straining body effort, the resistance against these infections has decreased. Vitamin C raises this resistance, as far as possible. One to two grams/day during periods of intense training and races seems suitable. When infections arise some doctors even prescribe five to ten grams/day.

- **Iron:** iron supplement is only significant if there is an iron shortage, i.e. at too low ferritine quality. Many cyclists systematically take iron preparations, even without a shortage being established. This, in the first place, makes no sense, and secondly it is not without danger for your health because the surplus to iron is piled up in the spinal cord and in organs such as the liver.

For the positive use of amino acids as a nutrition supplement, some directives must be observed:

1. Amino acids must be administered in correct and sufficiently large amounts.

2. It is recommended to take amino acids on an empty stomach to insure an optimum intake in the body.

3. An amino acid is only incorporated effectively in the body when it is combined with maximum one other amino acid.

General conclusion

1. Always drink sufficiently during training sessions, even in less warm weather. Make it a habit to drink approximately 20 cl every quarter of an hour.

2. Ensure enough fluid intake apart from training sessions.

3. Replenish the energy stores during intensive training sessions and races, preferably by means of energy drinks. Per hour 60-70 g carbohydrates must be consumed.

4. Always replenish energy stores after the intensive training sessions and races. Within 15 to 30 minutes after the training session/race, start using energy drinks. Try taking in approximately 100 g carbohydrates during the first two hours after the race.

5. After using the energy drinks, the muscles must be reactivated by means of meals having a high share of carbohydrates (bread, rice, pasta, potatoes)

6. Adjust the nutrition pattern as a function of training labor. The energy intake during recovery days must be significantly lower than during intensive training days or race days.

7. The nutrition products having a high share of carbohydrates have to be the main part of the whole nutrition composition.

8. Make sure that fat still accounts for 20% of the total nutrition pattern. It is wrong to systematically ban it from nutrition.

9. Consciously limit the weight increase during the relative rest period.

10. Gradually scale back the body weight to the ideal weight when overweight.

11. Never economize on the intake of carbohydrates during a diet.

Photo & Illustration Credits